EIGHTH NOTE  PUBLICATIONS

Motitus

Ryan Meeboer

Motitus is Finnish military slang describing the tactic of totally encircling an enemy unit but, in effect, meaning an entrapment or envelopment. This piece is composed to create the musical depiction of an army trapping its enemy in this circle. Using mainly the first seven notes learned in most method books, this piece is great to use with a beginning musicians, or to further develop the musicality of developing musicians.

The piece begins by establishing the mood through the use of strong unison patterns which moves into some simple harmonies. This is a great opportunity to teach students many musical concepts, including developing tone with higher level dynamics, balance, articulations, and keeping their timing through the combination of shorter note values and rests. This opening is used several times throughout the piece, so it is good to develop these skills right at the beginning.

Another teachable opportunity involves the main melody that is introduced at measure 11. Depending on the section of the song, this melody can take on many forms: at measure 11, it is to be played lightly and with a little excitement, at measures 19 and 47, it can take on a presence of strength and excitement, and finally at measure 39, it takes on a dark and menacing form. The music being played to support the melody in these sections should be played in the same style to support the feel generated by the melody.

Another good chance to work on tone control is presented at the end of the piece where all instruments are to play fortissimo along with accents and marcato. This is especially important when the higher pitched instruments are playing the long note at measures 55 and 56. Here, the lower pitched instruments, that are playing the opening motif, need to be the more dominant part.

Ryan Meeboer is a music educator, who obtained his degree through the Ontario Institute for Studies in Education at the University of Toronto. As a composer, he has written and arranged many pieces for concert band, jazz band, and small ensembles. His young band piece, *Last Voyage of the Queen Anne's Revenge*, has been well received by performers, educators, and audiences, and his pieces are starting to be found on festival and contest lists. As a performer, he has had experience in several groups, including concert and stage bands, chamber choir, vocal jazz ensemble, acoustic duets, and the Hamilton based swing group, "The Main Swing Connection".

Ryan began studying music at the age of seven through private guitar lessons. During his years in elementary and secondary school, he gained experience in several families of instruments. Focusing on music education and theory (including composition and orchestration), he attended McMaster University to achieve his honours degree in music. Ryan is currently a teacher for the Halton District School Board in Ontario, where he continues to compose and arrange.

Please contact the composer if you require any further information about this piece
or his availability for commissioning new works and appearances.

ryan.meeboer@enpmusic.com

ISBN: 9781771578097
CATALOG NUMBER: BQ221530
COST: $15.00
DURATION: 1:40
DIFFICULTY RATING: Easy
Brass Quintet

MOTITUS

Ryan Meeboer

MOTITUS

B♭ Trumpet 1

Ryan Meeboer

B♭ Trumpet 2

MOTITUS

Ryan Meeboer

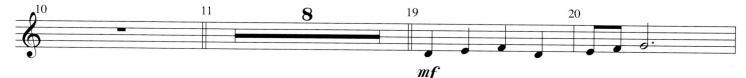

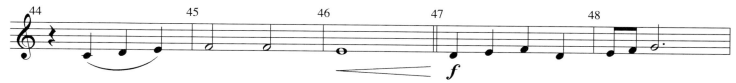

F Horn

MOTITUS

Ryan Meeboer

Trombone

MOTITUS

Ryan Meeboer

Tuba

MOTITUS

Ryan Meeboer

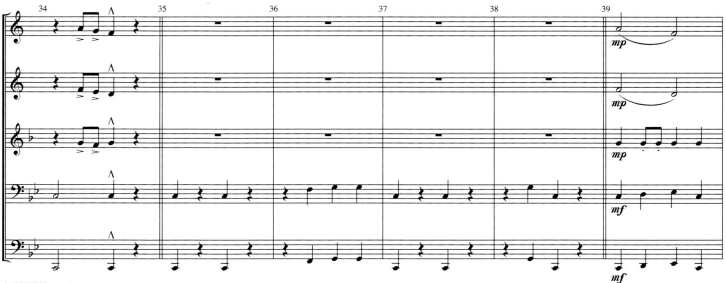

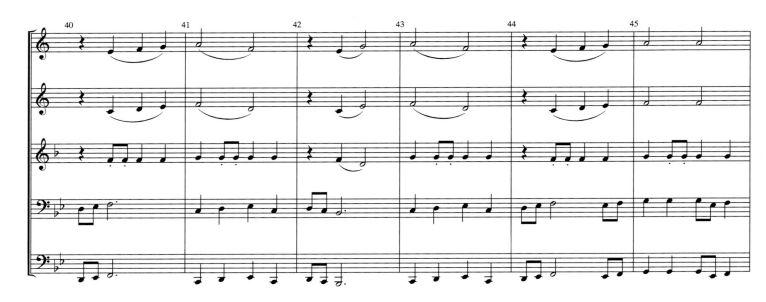